Bilingual Books Collection

California Immigrant Alliance Project

Funded by
The California State Library

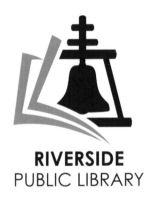

RIVERSIDE
PUBLIC LIBRARY

¡Mírame, ahí voy! / Watch Me Go!

MI BICICLETA
MY BIKE

Victor Blaine
Traducido por Eida de la Vega

PowerKiDS press.

New York

Published in 2015 by The Rosen Publishing Group, Inc.
29 East 21st Street, New York, NY 10010

First Edition

Editor: Sarah Machajewski
Book Design: Mickey Harmon
Spanish Translation: Eida de la Vega

Photo Credits: Cover, p. 1 spotmatik/Shutterstock.com; p. 5 Jacek Chabraszewski/Shutterstock.com; p. 6 Alinute Silzeviciute/Shutterstock.com; p. 9 KPG_Payless/Shutterstock.com; p. 10 fotum/Shutterstock.com; p. 13 lasalus/Shutterstock.com; p. 14 FXQuadro/Shutterstock.com; p. 17 Paul Vasarhelyi/Shutterstock.com; p. 18 (main) Aleskey Stemmer/Shutterstock.com; p. 18 (inset) pjhpix/Shutterstock.com; p. 21 Anton Gvozdikov/Shutterstock.com; p. 22 Monkey Business Images/Shutterstock.com.

Library of Congress Cataloging-in-Publication Data

Blaine, Victor.
My bike = Mi bicicleta / by Victor Blaine.
p. cm. — (Watch me go! = ¡Mírame, ahí voy!)
Parallel title: ¡Mírame, ahí voy!.
In English and Spanish.
Includes index.
ISBN 978-1-4994-0286-5 (library binding)
1. Bicycles — Juvenile literature. 2. Bicycles and bicycling. I. Title.
TL412.B53 2015
629.227—d23

Manufactured in the United States of America

CPSIA Compliance Information: Batch #CW15PK: For Further Information contact Rosen Publishing, New York, New York at 1-800-237-9932

CONTENIDO

CONTENTS

¿Tienes una bicicleta? Es divertido andar en bicicleta.

Do you have a bike?
Bikes are fun to ride.

Las bicicletas tienen dos ruedas.
Hay una rueda delante y
otra detrás.

Bikes have two wheels. There is
a wheel in front and a wheel
in back.

Las ruedas de las bicicletas también se llaman **llantas**. Las llantas se llenan de aire.

Bike wheels are also called **tires**. Tires are filled with air.

Las bicicletas tienen dos ruedas.
Hay una rueda delante y
otra detrás.

Bikes have two wheels. There is
a wheel in front and a wheel
in back.

Las ruedas de las bicicletas también se llaman **llantas**. Las llantas se llenan de aire.

Bike wheels are also called **tires**. Tires are filled with air.

Andar en bicicleta es sencillo.
Empuja los **pedales** con
los pies.

Riding a bike is simple. Push the
pedals with your feet.

Los pedales mueven la **cadena**.

- -

The pedals move the **chain**.

13

La cadena mueve
la rueda trasera.

The chain moves
the back wheel.

Andar en bicicleta puede ser difícil al principio. Puedes usar **ruedas de entrenamiento** para aprender.

Riding a bike can be hard at first. You can use **training wheels** to help you learn.

Las bicicletas tienen alrededor de 200 años. Desde que se creó la primera, ha habido muchos tipos de bicicletas.

Bikes have been around for almost 200 years. There have been many kinds of bikes since the first one was made.

El velocípedo es un tipo de bicicleta. Tiene una rueda grande delante y una rueda pequeña detrás.

Penny-farthings are one kind of bike. They have a big wheel in front and a small wheel in back.

Sea cual sea la bicicleta que tengas, ¡siempre usa un casco!

No matter what kind of bike you ride, always wear a helmet!

PALABRAS QUE DEBES SABER / WORDS TO KNOW

(la) cadena/
chain

(el) pedal/
pedal

(las) llantas/
tires

(las) ruedas de
entrenamiento/
training wheels

ÍNDICE / INDEX

SITIOS DE INTERNET / WEBSITES

Due to the changing nature of Internet links, PowerKids Press has developed an online list of websites related to the subject of this book. This site is updated regularly. Please use this link to access the list: www.powerkidslinks.com/wmg/bike